# INTRODUC

Patterned paste techniques can be used to create many different patterns such as swirls, dots, lines, checks, and combinations of all of these. Stunning and vibrant colours or soft, gentle background effects can be introduced into sugarpaste, marzipan or flower paste without the need for airbrushing, painting, stencilling, or petal dusting, saving the sugarcrafter many hours of tedious work. Moreover, if you like colour but are not sure of your painting skills, these techniques will enable you to introduce colour and vibrancy into your work without the need for painting.

Similar techniques for creating detailed patterns can be found the world over, in food like seaside 'rock', sweets, sushi, and also in crafts such as glass blowing and working with polymer clay. This book adapts these methods for sugarcraft, adding a few extra ideas along the way. The techniques will, I hope, inspire the creation of many more beautiful and dramatic sugarpaste cakes, open the way for an even greater range of sugar flowers and leaves, and provide quick and easy techniques for clothing marzipan models.

*Geraldine Dahlke*

Geraldine Dahlke

SPIRAL ROLL IN SUGAR

First published in March 2006 by B. Dutton Publishing Limited, Alfred House, Hones Business Park, Farnham, Surrey, GU9 8BB.

Copyright: Geraldine Dahlke 2006

ISBN: 1-905113-02-1

Publisher: Beverley Dutton

Editor: Jenny Stewart

Designer: Sarah Richardson

Editorial Assistant: Clare Porter

Design Assistant: Zena Manicom

Photography: Alister Thorpe

Printed in Spain

COMPOSITE PATTERN IN SUGAR

# CONTENTS

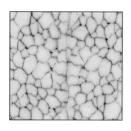

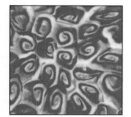

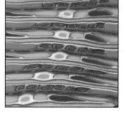

# GETTING STARTED

Illustrated step-by-step instructions for the basic techniques are included at the beginning of each section. These will provide the skills needed to recreate every variation in design. All patterns given are suitable for sugarpaste, marzipan, and flower paste – a guide to choosing and using different pastes and colours is given below.

Many more ideas and suggestions are given which can be easily made once you have learnt the basic techniques, and provide the inspiration for many works of 'sugar art'.

Always make small samples first to get to know the technique, and see if the colours you have chosen work well together.

Be adventurous, design your own version either by careful research, or just use happy accidents!

## PASTES

### Marzipan

The ideal paste for creating patterns as it colours well, is slow to dry, easy to use, and is naturally sticky. Marzipan is also the best paste to practise with! Choose a good quality, white marzipan with an almond content of at least 30%, such as Squires Kitchen Marzipan. This will ensure the colours stay true as well as giving superior taste.

### Sugarpaste

A good quality, ready-made sugarpaste is the best paste for covering a cake and can also be used to make every pattern, although sometimes it is advisable to add 10% flower paste (sometimes called petal paste) to increase its strength and help keep it moist for longer. It is advisable to strengthen sugarpaste in this way for backing pastes, patterns that take some time to make, and patterns that cover large areas.

### Flower paste

This can be rolled extremely thinly, so is ideal for flowers, fabric effects and other fine work. Once the paste has been kneaded and coloured, formed into a 'block', and stored airtight inside a food-grade, polythene bag it is ready to use for at least 24 hours. There is no need to knead the paste again before use.

There are a number of ready-made flower pastes on the market, all of which are suitable for creating patterns, so try different brands to see which you prefer. Squires Kitchen's Sugar Florist Paste (SFP) is a soft, moist paste that is ready to use and stays workable for a good amount of time.

# ESSENTIAL EQUIPMENT

Different patterns require different equipment, but there are a number of items that are used for most, if not all, projects so it is advisable to have them to hand before you start.

**Broad, soft paintbrush** (SK no. 10) – keep a brush solely for sugarcraft use and use to apply colour washes to pastes.

**Cocktail sticks** – these are extremely useful for dipping into paste colours and applying to pastes.

**Cooled, boiled water** – you will require a small amount for diluting paste colours. Do not use water straight from the tap as it may contain impurities.

**Cornflour duster** – you can dust the board with cornflour before rolling out flower paste to prevent the paste from sticking (see also white vegetable fat).

**Cutting wheel: small** – use this tool when cutting out shapes from paste, such as petals and leaves.

**Edible glue** (SK) – apply with a brush for moistening pastes and making them slightly sticky.

**Food-grade polythene bags** – small, clear bags (e.g. sandwich or freezer bags) are used to store paste and can also be cut into flat squares to cover and wrap around paste.

**Icing sugar shaker** – always dust the board with icing sugar before rolling out marzipan and sugarpaste to prevent the paste from sticking (never use cornflour).

**Non-stick polythene board** – essential for rolling out all pastes. Use the largest board you can.

**Non-stick rolling pins: large and small** – use the large rolling pin for rolling out large amounts of paste (e.g. when coating a cake) and the small one (approximately 15-20.5cm/6-8" long) for pattern making.

**Palette knife: small** – this will help to lift paste without distorting the pattern.

**Palette, saucer, or small bowl** – this is useful for mixing and diluting colours.

**Paste food colours** (SK) – a selection of colours is needed to colour pastes and make colour washes.

**Scissors** – keep a pair of fine scissors for sugarcraft use only.

**Sharp knife** – use a knife with a blade at least 5cm/2" long for slicing blocks of pattern.

**White vegetable fat** – always keep a small amount to hand for rubbing over sugarpaste and preventing it from drying out too quickly. This is also used to grease non-stick boards before rolling out flower paste.

# COLOURS

If you know which colours you will be using, ready-coloured pastes (such as sugarpaste and flower paste) are convenient and time-saving. However, if you are colouring your own paste or making colour washes, you will find that SK Paste Food Colours are ideal. A wide range of colours is available, including SK Hi Strength Colours, which are useful if a strong or dark colour is required.

## Colouring pastes

To colour sugarpaste, flower paste and most other sugar modelling pastes, dip the end of a cocktail stick into the paste colour and apply directly to the paste. Blend in thoroughly. To achieve a uniform colour in marzipan, colour a small amount first and blend this into the rest of the paste.

Flower paste may become very soft if large amounts of colour are added. Most sugarcraft suppliers stock ready-coloured pastes which are convenient, especially when strong colours are required.

Try not to over-work any paste, as this may cause it to dry out or, with marzipan, to become oily and crumbly.

TIP: always colour more paste than required as it can be tricky to match a colour if you require more paste.

COMPOSITE PATTERN IN SUGAR

## Making a colour wash

Using a wide, flat paintbrush, put some paste colour
into a paint palette (or similar) and add a little
cooled, boiled water. Mix together and test on a
spare piece of paste before applying to the pattern.

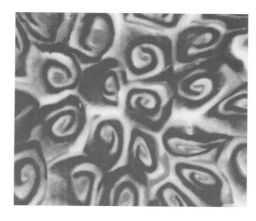

## Choosing colours

The colours to use for your patterns is very much a
personal choice. If you are unsure to begin with,
start by selecting two or three of the ones you like
best and see how they work together. You can also
use a picture or coloured object as inspiration for
more colour combinations: study it closely and look
for all the main colours as well as the subtle shades
and tones. Take note of all the colours that you
didn't expect to see, as these tiny highlights often
bring a colour composition alive.

Once you have planned all your colours, colour the
pastes before you begin making a pattern, and seal
in individual food-grade polythene bags. Arrange
them altogether and check the colour combinations
at this stage, before you begin. Always make a small
sample first to check the pattern, colour and tone,
and practise the technique. Trim off a small piece of
the pattern and keep as a reference.

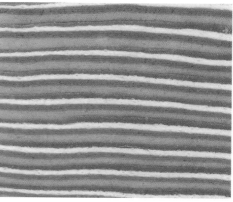

With careful planning, your patterned pastes
will almost certainly be successful, and
you will be rewarded with the joy
and satisfaction of an attractive
and uniquely decorated cake.

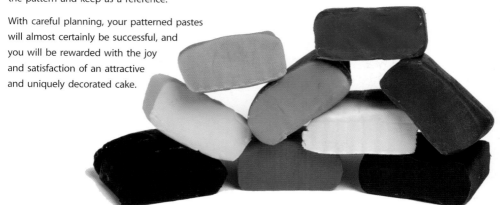

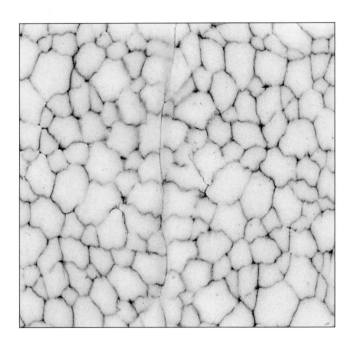

# SIMPLE ROLLS

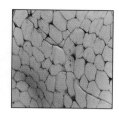

'Simple rolls' are sausage-like rolls of plain or patterned pastes stacked together lengthways to form a block, ready to be cut into thin slices like sliced bread. These slices are laid flat and fitted together on a backing paste, like a veneer. I would always recommend making a sample of the 'simplest roll' first, to become familiar with the basic technique.

## THE BASIC TECHNIQUE

### Preparing the paste

1. To make a sample, take a small amount of sugarpaste (approximately 90g/3oz) and mix in a little flower paste to strengthen it and increase its moisture content. About 10% flower paste to sugarpaste is a good proportion for all sugarpaste patterns.

### Creating the rolls

2. Cut the prepared sugarpaste in half and reserve one half in a food-grade, polythene bag ready for making the backing paste. Squeeze out all the air and seal the bag. Do not use clingfilm, as this is slightly porous and slowly allows the paste to dry out.

3. Colour the other half a pale colour using a hint of paste colour and cut into about six to ten chunks. Quickly form each chunk into a thick sausage or 'roll'.

### Reducing the rolls

4. Take each roll and quickly work backwards and forwards with your hands to make rolls

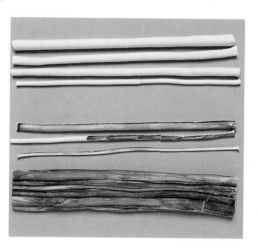

at least 17.5-20.5cm (7-8") long. The greater the variety of thickness the better, so do not aim to make them perfect. As you work, store all the rolls in a polythene bag.

### Painting

5. Dilute a contrasting paste colour with just enough cooled, boiled water to make a wash. Take out all the rolls and arrange them side by side on a non-stick board. Brush the colour wash

over the rolls with a broad, soft brush. This colours the rolls and also makes them sticky so they will bond together well when stacked.

## Stacking

6. Place the painted rolls together lengthways, making a long, thick sausage.

It is important to keep the rolls sticky so they bond together: if they are too wet they will slide apart, if they are too dry they will fall apart.

## Making a 'block' of patterned paste

7. Cut the large, composite sausage in half and lay one half next to the other, keeping the rolls all lying in the same direction. Squash the sides of the block inwards to exclude any air from between the rolls. Cut this in half again and lay one half on top to create a short, fat block with a large surface area of pattern at each end. Make sure there are no spaces between the layers by squashing the block inwards from all sides.

8. Wrap the block in a polythene bag, making sure the cut and patterned ends of the roll are sealed flat against the plastic to exclude

any air. Leave to rest for at least an hour, longer if possible, to allow the moisture to be distributed evenly throughout the block. This makes it much easier to slice and use.

## Preparing the backing paste

9. Lightly dust a clean, dry, non-stick board with icing sugar. Roll out the reserved half of sugarpaste into a shape approximately two thirds of the size required and a little thicker than the finished paste needs to be.

10. Gently smear a very small amount of white vegetable fat over the top and side surfaces; this prevents the paste from drying out too quickly and provides a tacky surface for the pattern to stick to. Make sure the paste is resting on enough icing sugar to prevent it from sticking to the table as you work.

## Applying the pattern

11. Dampen the top and sides of the block with the colour wash, just using enough to make it sticky, but not wet.

12. Using a sharp knife, carefully trim one end to leave a fresh, flat patterned side. (Store all trimmings in a polythene bag.) Cut another

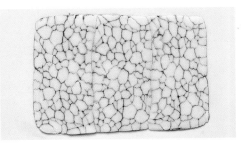

thin slice from the pattern and place onto the centre of the backing paste. The rolls should now appear as tiny discs. Continue to cut thin slices and place them onto the backing paste, butting the tacky sides against each other so they bond together without any gaps. Cover the pattern with a sheet of food-grade polythene as you work to keep it fresh and moist. Work quickly to cover the remaining backing paste with patterned slices.

## Rolling out

13. There are two methods for rolling out the paste, one to create an artistic, textured look and the other to create a smooth finish. To achieve a textured finish, roll out the paste gently to the required size, bonding the discs to the backing paste and evening out the thickness. Gaps will appear between the discs revealing the colour wash, and creating a lovely texture. For a smoother finish, gently massage the pattern together with your fingers to close any gaps, and then begin rolling out the paste. If there are any visible joins between the slices, roll the paste towards the lines from both sides to close them. Gently roll out the paste, keeping the pressure even all over to retain the pattern. (If a gap appears and refuses to close by careful rolling, place your hand underneath the gap to raise it up slightly and open it out, then carefully dampen the sides of the discs again using a small brush. Lower the paste down and the paste should stay closed.)

14. If a little moisture oozes out from between the discs, dab off with kitchen towel and then shake on a little icing sugar to finish drying the paste.

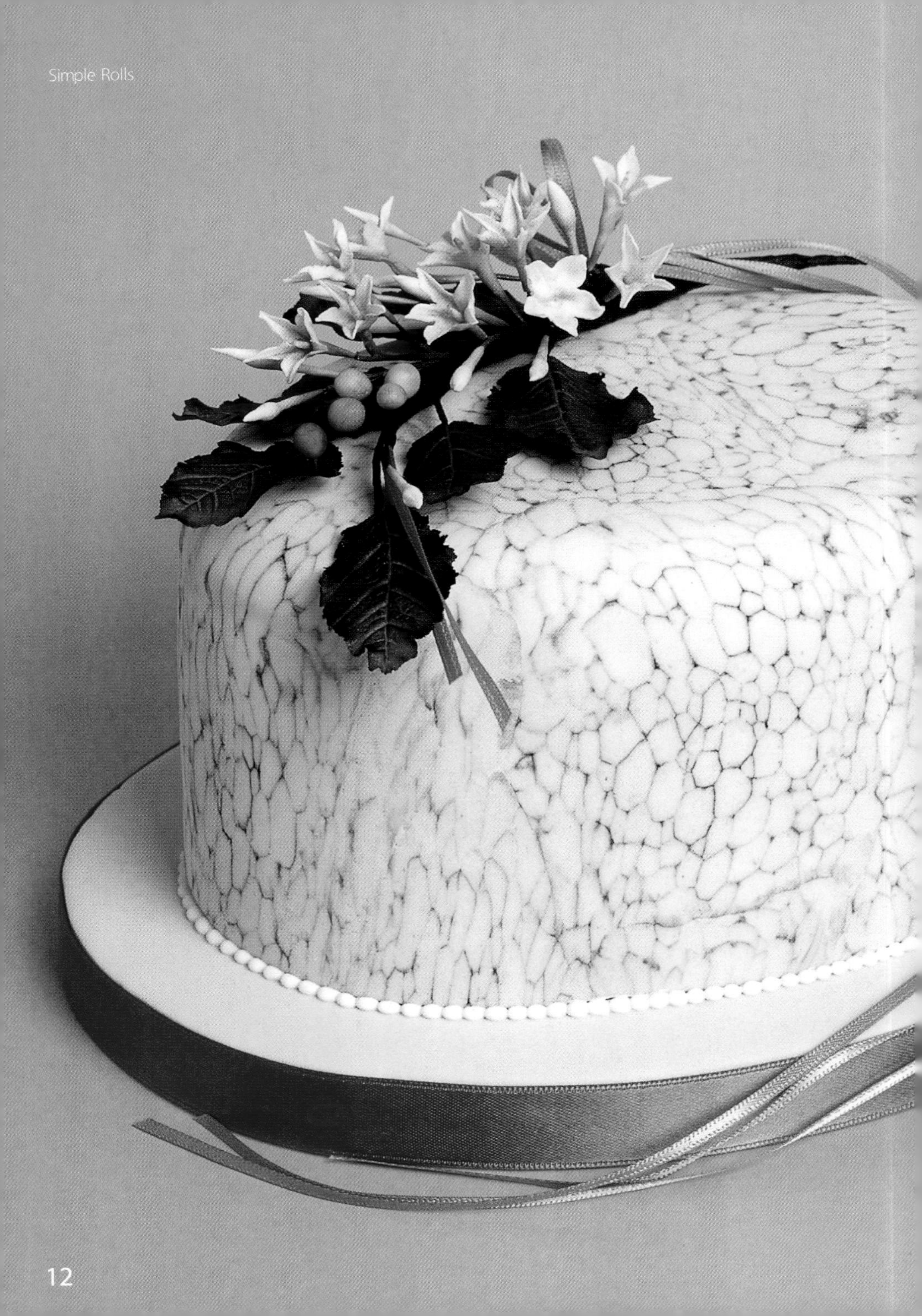

## Ideas for Using Simple Rolls

Once you have mastered the technique for making Simple Rolls, there are many ways in which you can use the patterned paste you have created. Here are a few ideas to inspire you:

• Use the technique for covering boards and cakes (see Coating a Cake with Patterned Paste on pages 46 to 47).

• Incorporate small pieces of patterned paste in plain sugarpaste coatings.

• Make a variety of different coloured rolls, then use them to create a multicoloured sheet of paste.

• Reduce some rolls more than others to create random and interesting shapes.

• Make a honeycomb pattern by packing rolls of equal size and thickness together very tightly and evenly. This will squash the rolls into hexagons.

• Using appropriately coloured sugarpaste and washes, make 'skin' for snakes and crocodiles, and leather for handbags.

• Create a leopard skin pattern by making rolls in black, brown and orange and omitting the colour in the wash, using just cooled, boiled water instead.

## Using the Trimmings

Once you have created a patterned paste, never throw away the trimmings! Store them in an airtight, polythene bag for future use. Here are some ideas for how they can be used:

• Blend the trimmings together to form soft, neutral tones. These can be used for coating the cake board, or can be added to other patterns.

• Add to a backing paste and use to coat a second, smaller cake.

• Keep all the trimmings (without blending them together) and wrap them tightly in polythene. Combine later with other coloured rolls to make Patterned, Complex or Composite Patterns (see subsequent chapters).

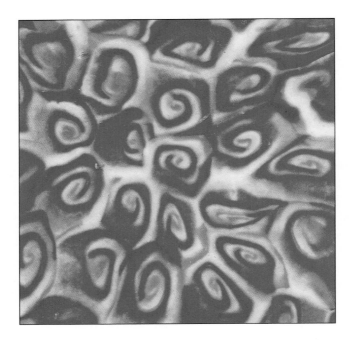

# PATTERNED ROLLS

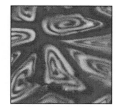

Designs from patterned rolls are really quite easy to make once you have mastered the basic simple roll. Whilst they can look delightfully complicated, in reality they are not.

Different coloured pastes are put together and formed into a large, fat roll that is reduced in size by rolling backwards and forwards until it is long and thin. (Surprisingly, the pattern is retained however thin the roll becomes, it just takes a little confidence to believe this at first. To check, cut across it and examine the cut end.) This long roll is cut into short rolls, which are then stacked, sliced, and placed on a backing paste in the same way as for simple rolls.

## TWO-COLOURED ROLLS

1. Colour some sugarpaste in two contrasting colours such as red and yellow, or in two contrasting tones, such as pale pink and red.

2. Make a short, fat sausage shape from one of the colours and moisten the surface with edible glue or cooled, boiled water to make it tacky, but not wet.

3. Roll out the contrasting paste into a rectangle. Roll the flat paste round the sausage and trim away any excess paste. Store the trimmings in a polythene bag, as before.

4. Reduce this sausage in size by rolling it back and forth into a long, thin roll. Cut into short lengths to stack and make a block.

5. Dampen the top and sides of the block, slice thinly and cover a backing paste as with the simple rolls. This paste can then be used in the same ways as previously described.

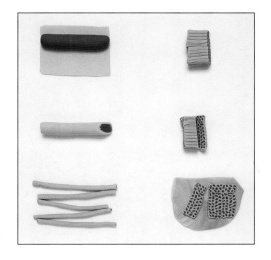

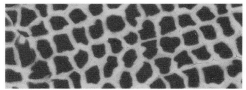

# MULTICOLOURED ROLLS

1. Prepare several different colours of sugarpaste. Roll one colour for a thin inner roll and moisten with edible glue or cooled, boiled water.

2. Roll out the remaining colours one-by-one. Roll up the sausage in a number of different coloured sheets of paste, following the same method as for the two-coloured rolls. Choose and arrange the colours carefully so they stand out against each other when reduced.

Lesley Bassett

# SPIRALLED ROLLS

1. Prepare two or more colours of sugarpaste. Roll each colour out thinly and cut into squares.

2. Stack two or more thin squares of contrasting coloured pastes on top of each other, dampening between each layer. Trim the sides.

3. Dampen the top surface and roll up the paste like a Swiss roll. Make sure the centre is solid, and not hollow. Roll out to a long, thin sausage to reduce the size of the pattern. Cut, stack and slice the pattern and apply to a backing paste, in the same way as for a simple roll.

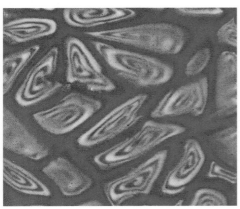

# MAINTAINING THE SHAPE OF A ROLL

As you work, you will probably notice the beautiful round rolls you have created get squashed and squared off when pressed together in a block: this can be either a happy design feature, or an annoyance, depending on the patterns you are trying to achieve. You can maintain their shape using this simple method:

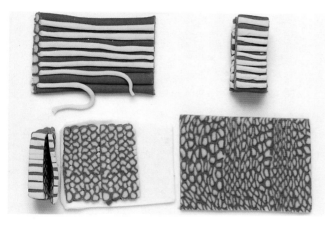

1. Prepare the rolls as required and place side by side on the board. Dampen them carefully and gently press together to form a wide, flat sheet.

2. Fill the depressions between the main rolls with tiny packing rolls.

3. Dampen the surface again, cut into sections and stack together to make the block.

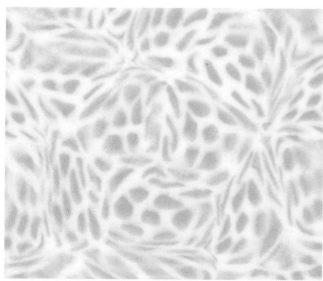

Packing rolls can become part of the overall design by using contrasting colours or smaller, patterned rolls, for example. Alternatively, by making packing rolls from the background colour (i.e. the last colour to be wrapped around the roll), they blend into the background and become invisible. When rolls are squashed together in a block, this outer colour appears as a background in the final pattern.

17

## Ideas for Using Patterned Rolls

The scope for creating different and varied patterns is enormous, so it is worth taking the time to experiment. Here are a few ideas:

- To create dots, make a two-coloured roll with a small cental core and a thick outer layer. Reduce, form into a block and make a sheet of pattern in the usual way. The central core will appear as dots.

- A cog wheel pattern can be created by coating a roll with a layer of stripes (see page 25) where one stripe is the same colour as the background.

- Use discs cut from spirals and multicoloured rolls for buttons, eyes, side decorations, or roll directly into sugarpaste.

- Try making multicoloured rolls with coloured sheets in a variety of thicknesses.

- Combine one, two, or more different patterned rolls to create a huge variety of patterned pastes.

- Reduce some rolls more than others to create slightly random, interesting patterns.

- Create patterned drapes and inserts by making a sheet of pattern then cutting out and using the shapes as required.

- Create ribbons by making a long block of pattern in Mexican paste. Cut off thin slices, roll out, trim the sides, and use to make into ribbons for draping over cakes.

- To produce delicate, feathery spirals or circles, use white or pale sugarpaste and roll out into a large sheet. Coat with a contrasting colour wash (see Simple Rolls, Painting on page 9). Roll up as for spirals or multicoloured rolls, reduce, and continue to create a sheet of pattern in the usual way.

- To create the illusion of circles, colour two thirds of the required amount of paste a background colour, and one third the colour of the circles. Begin with a roll of background colour in the centre, roll the 'circle' colour around this, and finish with a sheet of background colour around the outside. Stack together using the background colour to pack out the holes (see overleaf, Maintaining the Shape of a Roll). Cover a backing paste with slices in the usual way. Rolled out, the circles appear to float against the background as if they have been applied individually.

- Mix plain rolls with patterned ones, and the patterned ones appear like medallions in the finished sheet.

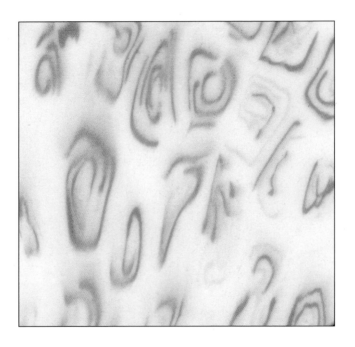

# COMPLEX ROLLS

These techniques are a little different from the rolls described so far, and offer a variety of patterns with only a small increase in complexity. However, if you have just dipped into the chapter and would like to try out one of the patterns, do make sure you have read and understood the basic techniques for simple rolls first.

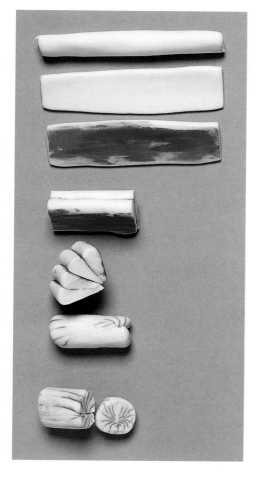

## THE WHEEL

1. Sprinkle the work surface lightly with icing sugar. Make a long, plain roll of sugarpaste in your chosen colour, about 1m (1yd) long, and lay it straight along the work surface.

2. Gently flatten one side with a rolling pin so that a cross section would look like a long, thin triangle. Paint a contrasting colour wash over this flattened side and rub the moisture in with your fingertips until it is tacky but not wet. Cut the roll in half and place one half on top of the other, to make a wider triangular shape.

3. Continue to cut the block in half and stack together until a semi-circle is formed. Slice the semi-circle in two and arrange in a circle. Glue together with colour wash, rubbing it in to make it sticky.

4. Roll the newly formed cylinder into a longer, thinner roll to reduce the pattern to the size required. Make sure the centre stays solid.

5. The wheel design can be used to form a block for a sheet of wheels, or cut into discs and used separately.

## Variations for the Wheel

- To make a two-tone wheel, make two long rolls in different colours. Flatten their sides as described overleaf and use cooled, boiled water to stick them together. Continue as before.

- For a multicoloured wheel, start with a number of different coloured rolls and stick them together with a coloured wash.

- For petal-like patterns in the finished discs, make a two-coloured roll (see Patterned Rolls on page 15) and use it instead of a plain roll, following the same method for the wheel.

- For a further variation, make a multicoloured roll (see page 16) and continue as above.

- Mix plain, two-coloured rolls and multicoloured rolls for intricate wheel patterns.

- For a wheel with a rim, make a two-coloured roll with the background colour (see page 17) for the inner core and a contrasting colour stuck around it. Use to create the wheel pattern, then add an additional layer of the contrasting colour around it to form the wheel rim. Finish by wrapping a thick sheet of background colour around this complete wheel and use either as a block of pattern or a medallion.

Risa Kuriyama

# OVERLAPPING ROLLS

1. Make two rolls in different colours, e.g. orange and red, and flatten one side of each as for the basic wheel. Dampen and make sticky the flattened surfaces with cooled, boiled water or a colour wash.

2. Place one colour on top of the other so the thin edges overlap in the middle.

3. Cut and stack to form a block where the red sides are always stacked on the red, and the orange on the orange. Trim the patterned face smooth and flat. Slice off a thin sheet of pattern and use to make petals (see tulips on pages 39 to 41) or squash the block until it is long and thin to make ribbons, bands, and drapes.

# FLATTENED ROLLS: ROSE PATTERN

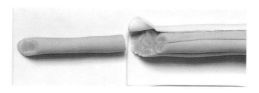

## Centre pattern

1. Make a large, three-coloured roll and reduce until seven equal sections can be cut. Combine these seven sections lengthways into one large, thick roll, remembering to stick them together with edible glue or cooled, boiled water. Stick a layer of background paste around this composite roll and store in a polythene bag.

## Flattened rolls

2. Make a two-coloured roll and lay along a non-stick board or work surface dusted with icing sugar. Using a large rolling pin, flatten along both edges, leaving a thicker 'spine' running down the middle. Dampen the surface all over with a little cooled, boiled water and rub in with your fingertips until the paste is sticky.

## Completing the pattern

3. Take the reserved roll from the bag and wrap the flattened pieces lengthways around it, overlapping each edge with the next. Slice into discs and arrange on a backing paste. Continue as usual.

## Variations for Flattened Rolls

- Use different types of rolls, e.g. spirals or multicoloured rolls, flatten and overlap to make interesting patterns.

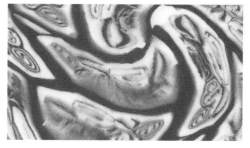

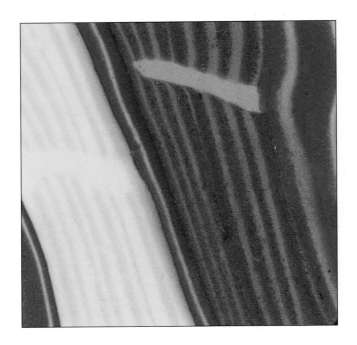

# STRIPES & CHECKS

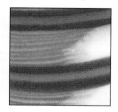

Striped and checked pastes can be used on a host of different sugarcraft items and are relatively quick to make using the methods shown here. The instructions given are for marzipan, an ideal paste to use for patterned work as it is naturally sticky and will stay moist for longer than sugarpaste. However, the same techniques can be applied to sugarpaste and other roll-out pastes.

## STRIPES

### Preparing the pattern

1. Colour two equal pieces of marzipan in contrasting colours or tones, such as black and yellow, or pale and dark blue. Form each coloured piece into thick squares and place one on top of the other.

2. Thin the squares by rolling or pressing them together.

3. Cut the squares in half and stack one on top of the other to form a block, keeping the cut edges one above the other. Thin the block again and cut and stack as before. Repeat this process until the stripes along the cut edge are a little thinner than required for the final design.

### The 'cut and flip'

4. Trim the cut edge of the block to give a clean, straight edge.

5. Cut a slice from this edge about 5mm ($^1/_8$") wide and, with the knife, flip this slice over onto its side so the pattern is facing upwards. Cut and flip a second slice and lay it alongside the first.

### Making a sheet of stripes

6. Butt these two strips together side-by-side to form one wide pattern. Continue to cut and flip strips, butting them together to create a sheet of stripes.

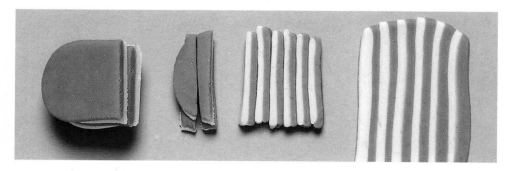

**Note:** marzipan is naturally sticky and will butt together easily. When using sugarpaste or flower paste, dampen and rub the moisture into the top surface of the block before slicing. When flipped, this tacky surface will bond the slices together.

7. Place the sheets of stripes on a backing paste as you work.

## Rolling out the stripes

8. Once a sheet of pattern is large enough, roll it out on the backing paste in the usual way. Rolling along the stripes will make them long and narrow, while rolling out across the stripes will make them short and wide.

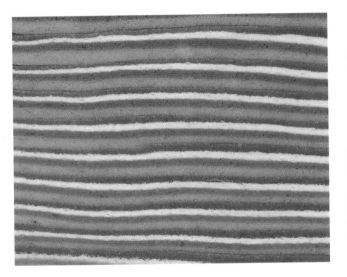

9. For thin pieces of pattern, place the marzipan between two sheets of polythene and roll out until the paste is as thin as required. Peel back the polythene and use for clothing figures, etc.

### Variations for Stripes

- Try using many different coloured stripes.

- Make stripes of different thicknesses.

# CHECKS

## Preparing the pattern

1. Begin by making two squares of marzipan in contrasting colours. Flatten them to an equal thickness and place one on top of the other. Trim one edge straight. Continue to make blocks of stripes, as described on pages 25 to 26.

2. Cut and flip 5mm ($^1/_8$") thick slices from this edge and form a sheet of stripes, as before. Place on a non-stick board sprinkled with icing sugar.

3. Turn the whole sheet round 90° so the stripes lie horizontally across the board, and then trim the side straight. Cut off a strip about 5mm ($^1/_8$") wide from this edge, which should appear as a long line of tiny squares. Keep this close to the cut edge of the sheet.

## Creating the checks

4. Place a spatula underneath the side of the sheet to support the cut edge. Lift it carefully and move the whole edge one square down the side of the 5mm strip. Line up the squares so they form a checked pattern and pull out the spatula, taking care not to distort the marzipan. Press or butt the strip back onto the sheet of stripes in its new position.

5. Cut off a second strip so you now have two strips of squares. Lift up the edge of the main sheet as before and this time move it up one square. Pull out the spatula and butt the cut sides together again.

TIP: it may be easier to move the strips up and down instead of the main sheet.

6. Continue cutting and moving the main sheet up and down in this way, creating a checked pattern.

7. Smooth the finished pattern by rolling a rolling pin gently across the surface, taking care to maintain the square shapes. Follow the instructions for rolling out stripes, steps 8 and 9 (see opposite).

Ryoko Onishi

Carole Evans

## Ideas for Using Stripes and Checks

By adding a little flower paste to marzipan or sugarpaste, you can use striped and checked patterned pastes in the following ways:

- to make ribbons.

- to make drapes.

- to make clothing for models.

- to use as inserts for side or top panels on a cake.

- to cover cakes and boards.

- to wrap round tea fancies.

- to create chess boards, paving stones, etc. on novelty cakes and marzipan models.

- to make striped Garrett frills by creating a block from Mexican paste, cutting off a slice and rolling lengthways to make a long ribbon before frilling.

## Variations for Checks

- Use four or six colours to form patterns of multicoloured squares.

- Cut strips of unequal thicknesses to vary the pattern.

- To make a herringbone pattern, use three or more colours and work up to step 3, the point where you move the sheet of stripes up and down to create the checks. This time, move the sheet of stripes up one square, three or four times in succession, and then down the same number of times.

- Make a more complex and interesting variation by including lines of contrasting stripes or squares between the strips in the finished pattern. Insert them during step 4, while butting the lines together to make the finished sheet of paste.

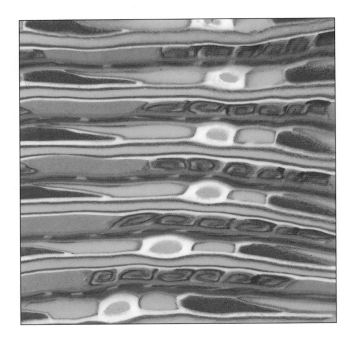

# COMPOSITE PATTERNS

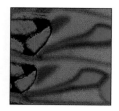

These are great ways to introduce colour and vibrancy into sugar pastes, as well as using up all the odd colours and patterns left over from other projects. However, choose which ones to use carefully so the end result is attractive.

## CREATING A COMPOSITE PATTERN

### Collecting the colours

1. Make or collect together a variety of coloured and multicoloured rolls, wheels, stripes and checks. Create more coloured rolls to balance these, such as plain, strong, or neutral colours, or combinations of all three. Store airtight in food-grade polythene bags until required.

### Assembling the block

2. The block will be made from many different pastes so will require careful handling to keep it together. It is usually best to build it on a square of paste so it can be picked up and handled easily. This base square will appear as a stripe in the repeat pattern, so its colour is important.

3. Roll out a square of suitable colour to the size the finished block will be. To prevent this paste from drying out, cover with a thin smear of white vegetable fat.

4. From the collection of patterned pieces, create a variety of shaped rolls, keeping some round, flattening others into ribbon lengths,

rolling a few into long triangles, etc. Dampen all the rolls with cooled, boiled water, a colour wash or both, depending on your design.

5. Measure the length of the base square and cut all the pieces to the same length. Arrange lengthways along the base, building up a block of shapes and colours. Fill in any gaps with lengths of plain colours to maintain the shape of the individual pieces.

6. When the stack is complete, press the top surface flat so there are no gaps. You may add another sheet of coloured paste here if you

wish to keep the block compact and easy to manipulate. Wrap completely airtight in food-grade polythene and leave to rest (see page 10, step 8).

7. Dampen the top and sides with a little edible glue or cooled, boiled water and rub in to make it sticky.

## Preparing a backing paste

8. Strengthen some sugarpaste for the backing sheet by mixing in 10% of flower paste. Roll out to two thirds the required size of the finished piece. Smooth a very thin layer of white vegetable fat over the top and sides to prevent it from drying out quickly.

9. Cut slices from the patterned block and cover the backing paste in the usual way. Roll over the pattern carefully, securing the pattern to the backing paste and making the surface smooth. Use the paste as required.

**ORGANIC PATTERNS**
**Brooklands College Students**

# DESIGN IDEAS USING COMPOSITE PATTERNS

Once you have made one or two composite patterns, you will be able to see how to control the shapes that make them up. There is huge scope for creating your own designs, so it is worth experimenting with different effects. Here, I have suggested a few ideas to inspire you.

## Wallpaper effect

1. Roll or flatten the block a little so when cut, the slices are long and thin. Dampen the top surface. Arrange the slices side-by-side across the backing paste like wallpaper on a wall.

2. Create slices like wallpaper and arrange in a wavy pattern.

3. Take the finished sheet of composite pattern and roll out in different directions to manipulate and change the original pattern. This is ideal for making use of a design that did not quite turn out as expected!

## Composite checked pattern

Take several different coloured rolls and press them into square-sided rolls before making a block. This produces fascinating patterns – use bright colours for sheets of vibrant pastes, or use shades of brown and grey to represent paving stones.

## Organic pattern

Construct a block from multicoloured rolls with many shades of green and small amounts of brown, red, orange and yellow.

## Fabric effects

1. Create rolls in the shape of stars, crescents, triangles, etc. Prevent the shapes from distorting by packing out the spaces along the rolls with contrasting or neutral colours.

2. Create flower-like patterns within rolls and use to make repeat patterns, like printed fabric.

# MAKING FLOWERS & LEAVES

Flower paste probably gives the sugar artist more varied and interesting ways to use patterned paste techniques than any other paste. The techniques described so far can be used to create many realistic and fantasy flowers, constructing the rolls, blocks and sheets from flower paste in the same way as sugarpaste or marzipan. Just take a little extra care to make sure the paste is tightly sealed in a food-grade polythene bag to keep it absolutely airtight and fresh.

Rolling out patterned pastes thinly for petals or leaves exposes an infinite variety of tones and hues as the colours begin to blend together, giving the sugarcrafter unique and often exquisitely patterned flowers and variegated leaves. Once a block has been constructed, a large number of matching leaves and petals can be made, very few requiring any further painting, airbrushing, or even dusting. There is only room in this chapter to describe a few simple examples, but I hope you will be inspired to create many more. The scope to make not only realistic, but amazing and fantastic fantasy flowers is infinite; just let your imagination run wild.

## WORKING WITH FLOWER PASTE

Once flower paste has been kneaded and coloured, formed into a block, and tightly wrapped in a polythene bag, it is ready to use for at least 24 hours. Provided there is no air present to dry out the paste, it can be worked without being kneaded again, so the pattern is preserved. Simply cut and roll out thin slices from the block and cut out the petal or leaf, leaving any dry, crusty edges behind.

## PATTERNED ROLLS: SIMPLE PETALS & LEAVES

### Simple filler or fantasy flowers

1. Make a two-coloured or multicoloured roll from flower paste.

2. Cut a disc from the roll, about 2mm ($^1/_{14}$") thick. Press a cone-shaped tool into the centre and work the paste round to form the centre of the flower, pulling the paste to the back to form the ovary (like a coned Mexican hat shape).

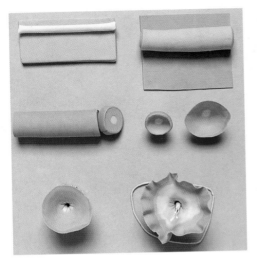

## Simple, two-tone leaves

3. Choose a suitable gauge of floristry wire for the flower you are making. Make a hook in the end and moisten with edible glue. Pull the wire down through the centre of the flower to embed the hook in the base.

4. Thin and shape the sides by pressing the paste between two fingers. Thin the edges further using a ball tool. Tweak into an interesting shape and hang upside down to dry.

1. Colour one portion of flower paste a soft, pale green, and another slightly larger portion a dark green.

2. Make a series of tiny, two-coloured rolls with the pale green on the inside. Form the rolls into a block. Turn the block so that all the rolls are lying vertically. Gently press down along the left-hand side of the block to flatten it slightly, and then press down on the right-hand side to match, creating an eye or leaf-shaped block.

3. Trim a thin, even slice of patterned paste from the top edge of the block where all the ends of the rolls lie. Roll out, following the direction of the pattern to keep its shape. Leave a thicker, central spine down the leaf for the wire. Cut out the desired leaf shape using a cutter, template, or freehand using a tiny cutting wheel.

4. Insert a suitable floristry wire a little way down the centre spine. Texture the leaf in an appropriate veiner (optional), then thin and soften the edges with a bone tool on a foam balling pad. Tweak the leaf into shape and leave to dry over crumpled kitchen paper or another suitable former.

> TIP: always make sure the block is carefully stored again as soon as each slice has been cut. Make sure the cut end is pressed against the polythene to keep it absolutely airtight, and twist the bag round it.

## 'Organic' leaves

1. For an organic pattern suitable for making amazing leaves, use flower paste to construct a block from multicoloured rolls with many shades of green and small amounts of brown, red, orange and yellow.

2. Cut slices from the block, cut out leaf shapes, wire and finish in the usual way.

# THE WHEEL TECHNIQUE: ROSES, CARNATIONS AND FILLER FLOWERS

Make a wheel pattern using coloured flower paste stuck together with a contrasting colour wash. Slice off 2-3mm discs and roll out very carefully, from the centre outwards to ensure the disc remains circular and the pattern forms the spokes of a wheel. Make into carnations, filler flowers, or use to cut out rose petals using a five-petal cutter.

To make more subtle roses, start with a roll constructed from sheets of different shades of pink and peach. Flatten the side of the roll and slice off small pieces, rolling these out to form individual petals. Alternatively, cut and stack to form a wheel. Slice off a 2-3mm disc and roll out, retaining the wheel pattern, and use with the five-petal rose cutter.

# OVERLAPPING ROLLS: ROSES AND TULIPS

Use this technique for flowers where the base of the petals are a different colour or hue, such as in some varieties of roses and tulips.

## Rose petals

There are many books available which describe in detail how to make beautiful and realistic sugar roses. Follow their methods using patterned petals made from overlapping rolls.

1.  Take two suitable colours of flower paste, such as yellow and pink, and make a block of overlapping stripes (see page 22). Cut off a slice about 2mm ($^1/_{14}$") thick and store the block in an airtight, food-grade polythene bag. Roll the slice out carefully, controlling the pattern by rolling in the direction you would like the pattern to go. (For a wired petal, remember to leave a thicker ridge down the centre.)

2.  Cut the petal out to the required shape using a cutter or a template. Vein the petal (optional) and thin the edges with a ball tool. Continue by following the method for the rose of your choice.

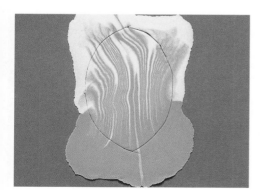

## Tulip

Tulips come in many shapes and some have very defined stripes on the petals. These instructions show how to make a simple globe tulip, a shape rarely found in sugar flower books.

1.  To make a former for a tulip petal, use a hard-boiled egg, an egg-shaped polystyrene shape, or even a small chocolate egg. Starting at the more pointed end, draw lines to divide the former into three equal segments, rather like an orange. Trace one segment onto tissue paper, rounding off the pointed ends to make a tulip petal template.

2.  Colour equal amounts of flower paste orange and claret. Make a block of overlapping stripes (see page 22) and store carefully, tightly wrapped in a food-grade polythene bag to exclude all air.

3. Twist a square of clingfilm tightly over the side of the egg shape. Fix the twist of clingfilm in place at the back of the egg with a little masking tape. Bend a narrow gauge wire a little way over the wide end of the egg to take the curve of a tulip petal.

4. Cut a slice from the prepared block and roll out with a central ridge. Cut out a petal with a tiny cutting wheel. Insert the curved wire, easing it gently down through the central spine. Lay the petal over the egg shape with the wire at the wide end. Ease the petal over the side of the egg, encouraging any excess paste to end up as gathers along the top of the petal. Trim to shape with a tiny cutting wheel.

5. Leave to dry for 24 hours. To prevent the egg from rolling around, rest it on a plastic bag half-filled with rice or sugar. Remove the petal by untwisting the clingfilm and gently pulling out the egg, then carefully peel the clingfilm away from the petal. Leave to dry.

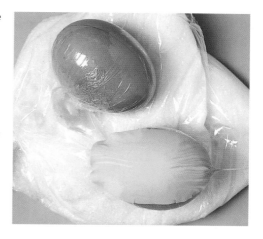

6. To create the tulip, make six petals, three slightly shorter than the others. Create the centre of the tulip with six handmade or commercially made stamens and wire round a central ovary. Tape the three shorter petals round this centre. Tape the remaining three petals round the inner petals, making sure the gaps between the inner petals are hidden.

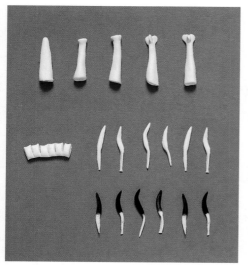

# STRIPES: PETALS AND LEAVES

## Striped petals

This technique is suitable for many flowers that have striped petals, from the 'Morning Glory' clematis to some varieties of camellias, tulips and lilies.

1. Stack up layers of coloured and white flower paste to represent the stripes in the desired petal. Roll or press the block to flatten it, cut in half and place one half on top of the other.

2. Continue to flatten, cut and stack the paste until the stripes are very thin. Always ensure that the layers are stuck together firmly.

3. Store the striped block airtight in a polythene bag. Cut slices from the block and make petals in the usual way. This technique allows you to make numerous identical petals without the need for painting.

### Additional ideas

- To create a petal with a delicate, feather-like stripe, use a pale-coloured paste and sandwich stripes together with a contrasting colour wash. Form into a block and leave for an hour or so, tightly wrapped in polythene, so the moisture is evenly distributed.

- For a more pronounced, coloured stripe, wipe a very thin layer of paste food colour between the stripes using your fingertip. Moisten with a little cooled, boiled water if necessary. Form into a block, seal in a polythene bag and leave for an hour or so to allow the moisture to be evenly distributed in the block.

## Striped Leaves

1. Colour one piece of flower paste a pale, yellowy green and another slightly smaller piece a dark green. Roll out both pieces, about 1mm thick for a small leaf and slightly thicker for larger leaves.

2. Make a strong, contrasting colour wash, such as red or violet, and paint over both pieces so they are tacky, but not wet.

3. Cut two equally sized rectangles from the dark green sheet and cut three more from the pale green sheet. Layer the pastes, beginning with a dark rectangle, followed by the three pale rectangles on top, and then finishing with the last dark one, tacky side down. Press gently to bond the layers together, but do not 'reduce' this block too much.

4. Trim along one edge of the block before cutting off a thin slice to roll out and form a leaf. The coloured wash will appear as delicate stripes along the leaf.

TIP: if the paste is too damp to roll, seal in a polythene bag for an hour or so to allow the moisture to soak into the paste a little. If, after this, it is still too wet, sprinkle a little icing sugar onto it to absorb any excess moisture. The sugar marks will disappear as you roll out the slice.

## 'Bendy' leaves

My thanks go to Sue Haskell of Brooklands College for teaching me her own way to make 'bendy' leaves. By incorporating the technique for stripes, you can create a colourful addition for sugar flower arrangements.

1. Start with a block as for striped leaves, but make it narrow, long, deeper, and brick shaped, not pointed.

2. Cut a slice from the long, thin side and flip over, with the best-pattern side uppermost. Roll out into one long, wide length on a non-stick board, taking care to retain the pattern. Cut in half across the centre, remove one piece and place this under a sheet of food-grade polythene for a few minutes. Turn over the remaining half and dampen this worst-pattern surface with edible glue.

3. Lay two thin floristry wires along this half, as if dividing it into thirds lengthways. Place the reserved half on top, best side up, and press down gently to join the two halves together. Trim to shape and soften the long sides with a ball tool on a foam balling pad.

4. Pick up the leaf in both hands, holding the wires as if they were handles, and bend it round to form a loop. (Bending the leaf over your fingers will make a narrower loop, if required.) Hold all four wires together at the base in a small bunch.

5. Pinch the base of the leaf together to neaten. Tape up the wires and the paste at the base of the leaf to form a neat stem. (Do not twist the wires or they will protrude through the paste.)

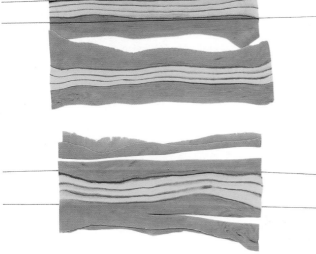

44

# COATING A CAKE WITH
# PATTERNED PASTE

When you first start making patterned pastes to cover cakes, it is advisable to start with small cakes, and gradually attempt larger cakes as you become more familiar with the technique.

## SEALING THE CAKE

First, prepare the cake as you would normally before coating with sugarpaste.

1. Spread the cake with a thin layer of apricot glaze, cover with marzipan and allow to firm overnight. Alternatively, spread a thin layer of buttercream over the cake (sponge cakes only) and leave to firm in the fridge.

2. If you have covered the cake with marzipan, dampen the marzipan with cooled, boiled water or clear alcohol (e.g. gin or vodka) just before coating with sugarpaste.

## PREPARING THE PASTE

Creating an attractive pattern in sugarpaste will take a little more paste than usual to cover a cake. Take the usual amount to coat the cake of your choice,

and add $\frac{1}{6}$ more to allow for the trimmings. The following table gives a rough guide to how much patterned paste you will need:

| SHAPE | SIZE | SUGARPASTE REQUIRED |
|---|---|---|
| ROUND | 15cm/6" | 400g/14oz |
| | 17.5cm/7" | 565g/1lb 4oz |
| | 20.5cm/8" | 660g/1lb 7oz |
| | 23cm/9" | 930kg/2lb 1oz |
| | 25.5cm/10" | 1.09kg/2lb 7oz |
| SQUARE | 15cm/6" | 565g/1lb 4oz |
| | 17.5cm/7" | 660g/1lb 7oz |
| | 20.5cm/8" | 930kg/2lb 1oz |
| | 23cm/9" | 1.09kg/2lb 7oz |
| | 25.5cm/10" | 1.19kg/2lb 10oz |

Sugarpaste is stronger, easier to handle and will stay soft for longer if approximately 10% flower paste is added to it. To make sure you add the right proportion of flower paste, simply divide the sugarpaste into 10 equal pieces and add a piece of flower paste the same size as one of these pieces. Blend the sugarpaste into the flower paste before use.

slices stick to each other as you arrange them. Cover the paste with a sheet of food-grade polythene as you work to help keep it fresh.

> TIP: for large cakes, prepare a block of pattern that will give you large slices to make the process quicker.

# USING THE BACKING PASTE

Always create your pattern on a backing paste. This seals the cake like any other sugarpaste coating, avoiding holes in the cake covering which may occur in the pattern.

Roll out the paste to $^2/_3$ the required size. Using your fingertips, grease the top and side surfaces with a very thin layer of white fat to prevent the paste from drying out.

# ADDING THE PATTERN

Starting in the centre and working outwards, quickly place the patterned slices on the paste (see page 10). These must be thin otherwise the extra weight might tear the backing paste when lifted. Remember to dampen the top and sides of the block so that the

# APPLYING THE PATTERNED PASTE

Roll out the paste to smooth out the pattern and join it together. The paste should now be rolled out to the size required to cover the cake.

Carefully lift the paste, supporting it with the rolling pin, and lower into place over the cake.

Occasionally, the pattern splits open as the cake is covered. This will not have any adverse affect on the cake itself as the backing paste seals it well, but it looks untidy. Try gently smoothing over the paste with your hand to close the gap. If this fails to work, leave the paste to firm and then pipe a little royal icing (coloured to match the paste) in the gap to fill it. Neaten the surface by wiping it smooth with your finger.

Remember to keep the trimmings for future use!

# STOCKISTS

**Squires Kitchen Sugarcraft**
Squires House
3 Waverley Lane
Farnham
Surrey
GU9 8BB
Tel: 0845 22 55 67 1/2
Fax: 0845 22 55 67 3
E-mail: info@squires-group.co.uk
www.squires-group.co.uk
www.squires-shop.com

**A Piece Of Cake**
Unit 18-19
Upper High Street
Thame
Oxfordshire
OX9 3EX
Tel: 01844 213428
Fax: 01844 214094
E-mail: sales@sugaricing.com
www.sugaricing.com

**Blue Ribbons Cakecraft Centre
and Party Parlour**
29 Walton Road
East Molesey
Surrey
KT8 0DH
Tel: 020 8941 1591
E-mail: blue.ribbons@talk21.com
www.blueribbons.co.uk

**CelCakes and CelCrafts**
Springfield House
Gate Helmsley
York
YO41 1NF
Tel : 01759 371447
Fax : 01759 372513
E-mail: celcrafts@btconnect.com
www.celcrafts.co.uk

**M&B Specialised Confectioners
Ltd.**
3a Milmead Industrial Estate
Mill Mead Road
London
N17 9ND
Tel: 020 8801 7948
Fax: 020 8801 4663
E-mail: g.scott@mbsc.co.uk
www.mbsc.co.uk

**Surbiton Art and Sugarcraft**
140 Hook Road
Surbiton
Surrey
KT6 5BZ
Tel: 020 8391 4664
Fax: 0870 132 1669
E-mail: sales@surbitonart.co.uk
www.surbitonart.co.uk

To see more of Geraldine Dahlke's work, log on to www.creativesugarart.co.uk.

For professional qualifications in bakery, confectionery, cake decoration and wired sugar flowers, full-time, part-time and evening classes, contact: **Brooklands College,** Heath Road, Weybridge, Surrey KT13 8TT. Tel: 01932 797700 Fax: 01932 797800 E-mail: info@brooklands.ac.uk www.brooklands.ac.uk

For a wide range of professional sugarcraft courses, Squires Kitchen International School is the largest independent School of Cake Decorating and Sugarcraft in the UK. For more information, log on to **www.squiresschool.co.uk** or call the Course Co-ordinator on 0845 22 55 67 1/2.